JANE YIN BOLANDER

7 PR Secrets All Founders Should Know

First published by JSY PR & Marketing, LLC in 2017

Copyright © Jane Yin Bolander, 2017

First Edition

*This book was professionally typeset on Reedsy.
Find out more at reedsy.com*

Contents

Forward

This book is based on an email series that my late wife, Jane Yin Bolander, wrote to help founders better understand Public Relations (PR). Her dream was to one day turn the series into a book when she recovered from leukemia. Unfortunately, she passed away on April 3, 2017 before she could turn her dream into reality.

As a tribute to her, I have decided to take her notes and publish 7 *PR Secrets All Founders Should Know* in her honor.

Jane's career spanned over fifteen years. Most of that was spent representing some of the most famous people in the world: Dontari Poe, Marshawn Lynch, Amare Stoudemire, Yao Ming, Lance Briggs, Anna Rawson, and Amel Larrieux, to name a few.

Later in her career, she expanded her business to help non-profits and startups harness the power of PR. Her particular passion was helping professional athletes with their non-profits that helped children. Like her life, she ran her business with a boldness, confidence, and integrity that her competitors respected and envied. She was an advocate for minority and women-owned businesses. She would often volunteer to coach and mentor women entrepreneurs. She had a particular passion for stopping human trafficking via her work with the Bay Area Anti-Trafficking Coalition (BAATC).

She was a wonderful person who was taken from us way too

early.

During her treatment, I stepped in to help her run her firm, JSY PR & Marketing. The experience was an invaluable education into the nuances of how PR works and why so many founders get it wrong – including me!

All the content in this book is based on her experience, notes, stories she told me, and what she taught me about the power of PR. My hope is that this will provide needed insights to founders who struggle to figure out how to use PR effectively in their organizations.

One final note.

Founders can be from any type of organization – be it for profit or not. The principles of the 7 *Secrets* are exactly the same. The only difference is in the end goals of the organization. While most of the examples will be about for-profit companies, the techniques apply to all sorts of organizations.

Thanks for keeping Jane's memory alive by reading and implementing the 7 *PR Secrets All Founders Should Know.*

Jarie Bolander
San Francisco, CA
August 2017

Introduction

Most founders think Public Relations (PR) is something that a college intern can do by using *MailChimp* to pitch to a list of reporters discovered on the Internet. It's usually the last thing a startup or founder or non-profit thinks of while building an organization. Even some notable startup publications think that hiring a PR firm for a startup is a vapid mistake. Vapid mistake! I actually had to look that up.

As a founder, you probably struggle to figure out when to do PR, what type of PR you need, and more importantly, how to go about getting your message out to the world. Don't worry. I wrote 7 *PR Secrets All Founders Should Know* for the founder who wants to understand how PR can help an organization and how to make the right decisions about who to hire and when to hire them.

In today's world, the lines between PR, marketing, and social media are blurred. Social Media has given founders the chance to promote their organizations without having to spend a lot of money; yet, founders often overlook a lot of opportunity by not exploring some of the more traditional, or not-so-traditional, PR avenues.

This book will explore those traditional and not-so-traditional PR avenues so that founders can get the maximum exposure for their organizations. I have used these secrets with lots and lots of startups, professional athletes, and non-profits. Some of these secrets revolve around how traditional PR techniques, like the press release, can be used to maximize exposure while others deal with what is actually newsworthy.

PR is all about getting your organization the best possible exposure so that customers or donors know how you can help them solve a problem. Essentially, you need to get people to know who you are, like what you are doing, and trust you enough to fork over their hard-earned money for your products, services, or cause.

Founders are unique in that they are trying to create a product or service or movement that has not existed before. This makes getting widespread attention a lot harder since traditional media channels may not fully understand how your organization is going to change the world.

Even publications like *TechCrunch* and *Fast Company* are hard for organizations to get into simply because there are always a lot of new and innovative organizations clamoring for coverage. In some cases, even getting covered may not give you the kind of exposure you were looking for.

My hope is that this book will give you an appreciation of PR and enlighten you about how you can use it to help grow your organization. At the end of most chapters, I have put a section called "Ways to Take Action Now!" This section will give you some insider pro tips on how to apply the secrets to your organization. These tips are what we use daily to help our clients get the exposure they want.

Part one details the 7 *PR Secrets All Founders Should Know* that was in the original PR series. I did update them from the original series to add some additional thoughts and the "Ways to Take Action Now!" section.

Part two is a *How to* section that did not appear in the original series. This content is exclusive to the book and will help you apply the 7 *PR Secrets* by helping you write your PR narrative, hire a PR company, pitch a reporter, and build your PR capacity.

I hope you enjoy 7 *PR Secrets All Founders Should Know.* PR has a lot of potential to help build your organization. I hope you take advantage of that.

Jane Yin Bolander
CEO, JSY PR & Marketing
San Francisco, CA
December 2016

I

The Secrets

"If I was down to my last dollar, I'd spend it on public relations."
– Bill Gates, Microsoft Founder

1

Secret #1: Not Everything You Do Is Newsworthy

When you own or run an organization, it's hard not to think everything is newsworthy and exciting. It's just like new parents, who constantly share pics of their babies. It might be exciting for family and friends to see all those photos, but when it comes to the rest of the world, it's not.

It's important to realize what is newsworthy and what is not because we want to spare you the "bad pitch." The more you pitch reporters a bad story, the higher the probability that they will blacklist you by blocking your email. Clearly, not a good thing.

Be Honest with Yourself and Be Useful

We work with clients who are constantly trying to get us to put out press releases about things that are simply *not* newsworthy. This has taught us that founders sometimes have a skewed view of what is newsworthy to reporters and the general public. It can be hard to separate yourself from your organization enough to take a look at it from afar and really be honest as to what the rest of the world might be interested in.

All of us know, deep down, what is interesting. It just takes some distance and perspective to realize that announcing something that happened a month ago is neither news nor interesting.

Reporters and bloggers are looking for interesting things to share with their readers. If you can be useful and give them substance that will help their readers be better or learn something, then that's a powerful and newsworthy story.

The Stranger Test

The most important test we use to determine if something is newsworthy is the stranger test. If you explained your potential newsworthy event to a total stranger sitting next to you at a cafe, what would happen? I know that this may seem simplistic but countless founders don't apply this simple test.

Part of what makes something newsworthy is that it educates and/or enlightens the reader. Again, think how your story can be useful to your cafe companion.

For those of you who still need a little more clarity on newsworthiness, consider what is *not* newsworthy:

- You had a meeting with someone
- You are attending a conference or event
- Announcing something that has already happened
- New hires, unless they are high profile executives
- Boring contests

If you can't remove yourself and your opinions from the equation (and please be honest about this!), then ask two or three other people in your inner circle who will give you an honest opinion. Please don't ask your mom or grandma. Both will most likely think that whatever their wunderkind comes up with is fantastic.

Make Your Own News

The good news is that if you're craving some PR, and you can't find a single thing that is newsworthy, you can still make your own news by creating it. Yeah, I know, sounds shady and all CIA Covert Affairs but there are things that reporters want to cover and that can be done easily. Some ideas include:

- Throw an event
- Release a new or revised product or service or capability
- Donate to or support a charity
- Product giveaways
- Come up with a clever social media campaign
- Conduct a survey with credible source on a hot topic
- Create an eye-catching infographic.
- Celebrate a company key milestone like user numbers, etc.

Reporters might want to cover your organization if your story is interesting and relevant. Make it easy for them to cover you by having materials readily available to make their job easier. For example, have an updated press kit and really good presence on search engines like Google.

It's important that you take a hard look at what you want to announce and make sure it's truly newsworthy. The more you cry wolf with bad pitches, the more people will ignore you.

Ways to Take Action Now!

1. **Build a Story about Your Organization:** Stories move us to action. Humans have told stories for thousands of years – so it's in our DNA. Do the PR narrative exercise in the *How To* section and build stories around that to share.
2. **Follow Reporters on Social Media:** Pick ten reporters who cover your industry and follow them on social media. Keep track of what they report on. Share and retweet their stories to build rapport.
3. **Publish Unique Data:** Periodically, publish some unique and interesting insights from the data you collect from customers or donors. This is a great way to be helpful and an expert.
4. **Speak at Events**: If someone reaches out to you to speak at an event, do it. Speaking at events will give you a tremendous amount of credibility and exposure when others search for you.

2

Secret #2: The Press Release Is Dead

Well, not exactly, but close.

Whenever our PR firm is hired by an organization, the staff are eager to see the press releases we will produce for them. Then we tell them that the press release is dead. Our clients have a hard time wrapping their heads around this. So we explain to them that almost no one is excited about getting an email press release sent to a mass audience. If your job is to write the next new, exciting story, would you be sold by that mass email?

DUH! No!

So the press release is not *really* dead. *But* it is not the same tool it used to be.

The Press Release Is No Longer Elite

Back in the old days, you needed to have the secret decoder ring to get a press release out on the wire. You also had to have a lot of money and influence to ensure that it got to the right place. Not anymore.

The means of distributing a press release nowadays is both

cheap and easy. Sites like Press Release Jet, Newswire, and PR Newswire make it really easy. Selecting the right service can be tricky since there are several free and paid services to choose from.

Let's just say that the press release has been resurrected as a side tool; but the main tool is the pitch. Master the pitch and you will win over all the reporters over. More on that in chapter 10.

The Makings of an Effective Press Release

There are a lot of great resources on writing a great press release, so I won't bore you with all nuts and bolts about creating a great headline, use hard numbers, make it grammatically flawless, or including quotes where possible. What we will cover is how to make your press release as effective as it can be.

If you recall, the whole point of PR is to get the word out about your organization and have the press cover you. The press release is the proverbial tip of the spear that gives the world a taste of what your organization is all about. It's also an important part of your Search Engine Optimization (SEO) strategy since Google and Yahoo crawl all the press outlets looking for content.

In order for press releases to be the most effective, make sure you have the following:

- **Up-to-Date Press Kit**: Press kits should be easy to find on your website. Don't have one? We'll need to fix that.
- **Social Media Consistent with the Release:** After you do the release, your social media should be consistent with the message. Don't jump the gun on this because anything done before the release makes it not newsworthy.

- **Good SEO via Content Marketing:** Reporters need to be able to find your company and story via Google. So make sure to have good content on your organization's blog (or website).
- **Up-to-Date Website:** Make sure the latest contact info and product information. I can tell you countless stories about organizations that failed to do this simple thing.

You Need to Think Beyond the Press Release

In a vacuum, the press release is not that effective. What a press release can do is spark interest from outlets that your social media or other media efforts can't or don't normally reach. This means your backup materials must be easy to find. That's why its essential to have an up-to-date press kit, good SEO (via content marketing), and a social media message that is consistent with what you are releasing. It's vital that a press release is only used to focus on what can be backed up by multiple sources of information.

Think about that for a minute and you will realize that most reporters or industry analysts are looking for multiple sources of easily obtainable and credible information in order to cover your organization. The press release is actually one of the least creditable because it's released by you and not necessarily vetted by others. Now, a good press release will be credible but the other sources need to back it up.

Ways to Take Action Now!

1. **Build an Editorial Calendar**: Take a look at the next three months and figure out what launches or news or events might be coming up. From those events, work back to when you'll need to pitch the press or develop materials.

2. **Find Places to Guest Post:** It's always a good idea to get on as many media outlets as you can. This means getting your executives to write pieces to publish on other sites.

3. **Build Press Release Templates:** Make sure to have approved templates for all the types of press releases you may want to publish. This makes it super easy to bang one out when needed.

4. **Pick a Service:** Choose a press release service ahead of time so you know exactly how it works. You don't want any surprises when you are on a deadline to make things happen.

3

Secret #3: Not All PR Is Good PR

Many people have claimed that "there is no such thing as bad publicity." If you're a founder of an organization, and you're looking for PR, I'm here to tell you that that statement is simply not true. Bad publicity can crater your organization. Just look at Elizabeth Holmes and her company Theranos and you'll start to see that bad press can ruin your organization.

But let's dig a little deeper into this concept and talk about how bad press can impact you and your organization. You can't always avoid bad PR, but there are some pitfalls founders can avoid to not get bad press.

Stay Away from Bad News and Sources

Don't try to glam on to someone else's negative PR even if you want to help. It's easy to want to do every media interview, especially when it's for a high profile media outlet, but always check to see what the opportunity entails before agreeing to it. Some media outlets have an agenda (duh) and being associated with them can lead to complications when doing business in other countries, companies, or other organizations.

Always Get the Story Straight

One time, one of our client was asked to be quoted in an article about how hard it is to raise funds in the current economic climate. Because the interview was with a major media outlet, the client immediately agreed to do the interview. They should have checked with us first. The article came out and the quote was manipulated. It looked like our client was complaining about their fundraising and struggling to raise funds. The short quote and the negative association it made deeply hurt our client's fundraising possibilities. Remember that investors, competitors, customers, and donors will Google you.

Spinning Bad News into Good PR

Most founders tend to sugar coat bad news and try to spin it into good news. Elizabeth Holmes over at Theranos tried to do just that on *The Today Show.* After that interview, things got even worse with the *Wall Street Journal* reporting that Theranos would void two years of blood tests and the DOJ wants to ban Elizabeth Holmes for two years from running a lab. Not to mention that the SEC has an open investigation into fraud. What a mess.

Now, contrast that PR nightmare with an equally nightmarish situation one that involves lots of money and a high profile figure. Meet Martha Stewart.

What's different about Martha Stewart is that she took responsibility for her actions (she got caught in insider trading). Owned it and got punished for it. Even during her five-month prison sentence, a *Time* magazine piece even quipped that "Martha Stewart's Prison Time Actually Helped Her Business." You go M. Diddy.

Ways to Stay on the Good Side of PR

It's best to always be on the good side of the press. It just makes your life a helluva lot easier. Here are a few helpful ides to keep you on the good side of PR:

- **Don't Rant on Social Media:** I know it's tempting to right a wrong by leaving a zinger of a comment to put some troll in his place. Believe me when I tell you, it's not worth it. If you have any kind of brand equity, it will evaporate fast if you pick fights with trolls.

- **Always Take the High Road with Customers and Donors:** Customers talk and they talk a lot when they feel they have been wronged or slighted. Donors do the same thing. In the end, a bunch of bad customer service PR will spiral out of control at some point when you least expect it. Unless you're like Pizzeria Delfina, which turned all their bad Yelp reviews into tee shirts and positive press, or the Utah Jazz on the nightlife in Utah. PR operator, master level.

- **Be Ethical in Your Business Practices:** This goes without saying, but I'm including this because so many people apparently aren't ethical. If you are an asshole, bad PR will find you. Remember that grade-A asshole, Martin Shkreli, who jacked up drug prices? It's almost like he wanted the government to arrest him.

- **If It's Too Good to Be True … :** When things get tough, some founders might want to try creative approaches to save their organizations. It's a noble cause, but if you are thinking of pulling a John Delorean. Always remember that the coverup is worse than the event, unless you get caught up in a $24 million cocaine deal — that's just bad all around.

13

- **Be Genuinely Helpful and Thoughtful:** It's important that others find your organization helpful and thoughtful because this translates into goodwill. Goodwill can translate into excellent PR when some crisis or event happens where a calm, rational person is required to comment. Because of your built up goodwill, clients and the press will give you the benefit of the doubt when something bad happens.

If the above is too much to remember, then remember what one of my old bosses used to say to me about PR. It's an oldie but a goodie. *If you don't want your grandmother reading about it in the paper, then don't do it.* Sage words to live by.

Ways to Take Action Now!

1. **Contribute to Forums:** Spend some time on industry forums to offer advice and resources. It's always time well spent to help out your community. People will remember that.

2. **Sign Up for Help A Reporter Out (HARO):** Reporters are always working on stories and HARO is a service that allows them to ask questions about all sorts of things. Like contributing to forums, helping a reporter is something that they will remember. Nothing gets on a reporter's good side like helping him or her out - massive karma points for that.

3. **Share Other's Work on Social Media:** It's important that you and your organization share content from other people online. This is a great way to get dialed into your market and community.

4. **Respond to the Community on Social Media:** Be sure to

address both good and bad feedback on social media. If you make a promise, such as refunding a client who received a faulty product, then follow through with your promise.

5. **React to Stories Happening on Social Media Now:** If you see a story that's compelling or aligned to your mission, take action and reach out. This might include giving away free product or helping someone get something done.

4

Secret #4: The Founder Is Different than the Organization

I'm also a founder of my own organization, and trust me, when you're so close to the nitty gritty of daily operations, sometimes it's hard not to feel like you and your organization are synonymous. When it comes to PR, it's vital that you separate yourself from your organization. That's because aspects of who you are might not be compatible with aspects of your company.

Many founders have been sucked into the cult of personality and cratered their organizations. Organizations have also fallen into this trap. Just ask Apple.

Separation between founder and organization does not need to be absolute, but there should be a healthy distance. It's vital to know where one ends and the other begins or the outcome will be bad for everyone. Just ask every Enron employee and shareholder.

The Founder and the Organization

Apple is a prime example of an organization that was defined by Steve Jobs. The two were inseparable even when Steve left. While this made Jobs an iconic leader and person that many people wanted to emulate, it left the organization (now under the capable hands of Tim Cook) in a bit of an identify crisis.

The leader of an organization is important but it's not only the charismatic leader that makes magic happen. It takes a dedicated staff of co-founders and others to make the vision a reality. A founder that recognizes this will build a deep bench of people who can step up when needed and talk to the press.

Share the Love

While it's great to have one spokesperson, sometimes you can't be everywhere. So you should share the love. It doesn't hurt for others on the team to understand the art of PR anyways. You never know whom your staff or management team will be talking to when they are out in the wild. It's better for them to all be prepared to talk to press, rather than hoard the press all for yourself. Forewarned is fore-armed.

All founders should be in the PR mix. It shows depth and breadth in the companies bench. It also adds more diversity and that's a great thing. Founders that hoard the spotlight will do themselves and their organizations a great disservice. Rumors will get around that so and so is a control freak and then people will avoid covering you. They might even put out rumors or bad stories.

Training Up So You Have Depth on the Bench

Training your executive or founding staff to be in front of the camera is not that hard. Media training should be part of any executive's assent to the top. Media training does not need to be something that's worked on daily. Rather, there should be some method to the madness and practice to stay sharp. Here are some quick and easy ways to get and keep your staff media sharp:

- **Brown Bag Talks:** Brown bag talks are great to build your presentation skills in a safe environment.
- **Organizational Meetings:** Let others give updates for their departments at an organizational meeting
- **Toastmasters:** Start a toastmasters club at your office or join a local one. Toastmasters is a great way to get feedback on your speaking skills and nervous ticks. If the camera adds twenty pounds, it also amplifies your ticks.
- **Conferences:** Send your co-founders or staff to a conference to present on behalf of the organization. Usually, the pressure is not that great and most people are supportive.
- **Formal Media Training:** Consider hiring a PR professional to train your staff. There is nothing like a seasoned PR pro to tell you the dos and don'ts.
- **Media Appearances:** Occasionally, have your co-founder or staff do an actual media appearance, especially if the appearance is among friendlies or is low-risk. This is an awesome way to build up their confidence.

Training your staff to handle the media will only help you. When co-founders and senior staff know what to say and how to say it, it makes the whole organization, and especially you the founder, look great. Also remember to be humble and remember that great scene from *Bull Durham* that all you want to do is help the ball club and you and your staff will do fine.

Ways to Take Action Now!

1. **Sign Up for a Conference:** Pick your favorite conference and sign up to go. Better yet, ask them if you can lead a discussion or give a talk. Don't delay. Do it today!

2. **Buy Your Senior Staff a Personal Development Book:** Set the tone for the behavior you want to see by buying your staff a book that helps them develop as professionals. This can be about public speaking or about how to communicate better. In fact, why not give them this book?

3. **Learn about Your Staff:** Understanding what your staff does outside of work can be a great source of interesting content that can cross over to your business, especially if they raise money for causes they believe in or volunteer their time for worthy causes.

5

Secret #5: You Really Do Need a Press Kit

What is a press kit? Sometimes also known as a media kit, it includes information and resources for reporters and sometimes investors to gain insights about your company in a clear, succinct way. A press kit usually includes high-level details about the organization, important past articles, logos, high-resolution images and video demos.

There are various frames of thinking when it comes to a press kit. In the past, people would build a physical press kit filled with print copies of media clippings, a "one-sheet" about the company or product and maybe a physical product sample. These press kits would be sent to reporters for consideration of coverage. As you can imagine this was costly, but sometimes those fancy press kits really made a difference for the type of coverage you got for your client.

The New Economy Press Kit

Of course, times have changed greatly. Everything lives on the inter-webs. So should your press kit.

The biggest reason why you need a press kit is because it gives you another level of legitimacy. Every organization should have some form of press kit even if it's short or doesn't have many media articles in it yet.

The press kit will show that you are serious and it makes a reporter's life easier. Reporters will make fewer mistakes because they will have all the details clearly spelled out and readily available. Reporters hate having to do Google search after Google search to find basic information.

There are quite a few online tools that can be used to create a press kit. Some of the ones I have used include: Storyboard (paid), Tackkh (free), and Presskit (paid).

You can also do something in Google Docs or directly on your website. We recommend that you put your press kit on your website so it's easy for the press to find and so that you get good SEO karma. At a minimum, post a link to one of the tools above on your Press page. Don't have a Press page. Geez, we got lots of work to do!

Components of a Stellar Press Kit

As I mentioned before, a press kit shows that you are serious and want to make a reporter's life easier. A press kit needs to be rich in information and visuals so it's Sesame Street simple to find what people are looking for. The essential components include:

- **Logos:** Use high-resolution logos with a description of the proper way to place them. Also make sure the logo is on a clear background and in multiple formats.

- **Organization Overview:** Display what your organization does, how big it is, what industry it is, etc. This is your elevator pitch.
- **Product or Programming List:** Provide a list of the products or services or programs you offer.
- **Key Staff List with Short Bios:** Include the bios of the management team and key people in the organization. Also have high-res head shots.
- **Product Images:** Display high-resolution product images with names that make sense.
- **Press Coverage:** Point to news stories, blog posts, and press releases all organized in chronological order with the most recent first.
- **Organization "One-Sheet":** Provide something that is more in-depth than the organization overview. Include details like mission, vision, etc.
- **Contact Info:** Share the names, telephone numbers, and emails of the media and marketing people in your organization.
- **Client Testimonials:** Show how much your customers like your product or how great your customer service is.

Don't worry if you don't have everything right away. A good press kit evolves over time, but it should always be up to date given the status of the company.

I know I sound like a nag but this happens way too often to not mention. It's important to have your kit done ahead of time and keep it updated. Nothing will turn off a reporter faster than an outdated press kit with old bios, stale products, poor quality images, and antiquated press. Your press kit is within your control and making it shine will tell the world that you are ready for the big leagues.

Ways to Take Action Now!

1. **Create Your Press Kit:** You must have known that this would be numero uno! Pick a platform and go make it happen.
2. **Schedule Monthly Updates:** Right now, go into your calendar and schedule a one-hour meeting each month to update your press kit.
3. **Reach out to Customers/Donors for Testimonials:** Call up your favorite customers or donors and ask them for a quote. Most people would love to help out if they like what you are doing.

6

Secret #6: Timing Is Everything

Chances are you have never heard of a Zune. Zune was the New Coke of MP3 players that Microsoft launched to try and compete with Apple's iPod. It was an attempt to capture the lucrative MP3 player market and it failed miserably.

Your stories, product launch, or announcement can have the same fate as the Zune if you don't figure out the right timing, the right audience, and the right channel to get the word out. The Zune was an extreme example of bad timing, but I bring it up for one important reason — all the signs were there that the Zune was not going to go well.

Do Your Home Work

The Zune is a classic example of a product (and narrative) that was trying to play catchup with an already entrenched offering from Apple. What this teaches us about timing is that no matter how big you are, no matter how much money you spend on promotion, or how great you think your story and/or product and/or cause is, if the story has already been played out, then it won't fly.

Reporters want stories that will captivate readers and get them to click and comment. If the mood of the country has shifted away from certain topics, no amount of stellar pitching or money will bring it back from the dead.

You need to ask if the reporter is looking for this story. In the case of the Zune, the initial launch story is news that someone is going after the iPod. What did reporters end up writing about?

The only stories reporters wrote about the Zune was how much of a failure it was. Reporters compared gave Microsoft zero slack. If the goal was to make a complete flop – mission accomplished!

Just remember that not everything you do is newsworthy. You should always consider how things can go wrong when pitching a story. That's why it's important to do your homework and pitch the right reporters the right story at the right time.

Consider these essential items a must for any pitch homework:

- **Trending:** Is the topic you want to release trending in the news or in your niche? Trending news always gets picked up quicker.
- **Reporter Fit:** Reporters have beats that they cover, which means they only cover certain topics. Make sure that the reporters you pitch actually cover your topics.
- **Buzz Worthiness:** All news has a buzz factor. Make your pitch and story more buzz worthy by offering exclusives or insights that are ahead of the news curve. Reporters love a good scoop.
- **Competing Stories:** Are there other stories that are dominating the news that are more important? If so, your story might get lost in the noise and not get the reaction you were looking for.

A lot of this is subjective and based on experience and the relationships you have with reporters. Don't get discouraged if you don't get hits right away. Sometimes timing is out of your hands. One other thing to consider is warming up before you pitch the big news outlets. Many an over-anxious PR rookie has pitched something too soon without first warming up their pitching chops.

Strike While the Iron Is Hot

Once you have an idea for a story and done your homework, it's essential that you don't delay in pitching and following up with reporters. No matter how good a story, if the timing is off, nothing will happen. Reporters are constantly on deadlines and they lose interest in stories quickly or will jump on trending topics without blinking an eye if the story friction (e.g. too hard to research) is too great.

Another thing to keep in mind is that reporters are on a constant deadline. They always want to rapidly develop a story, get it out in the world and move on. The typical story development cycle is less than a week, so getting the timing right on all aspects of a story (pitch, background material, etc.) makes it that much more likely that your story will get picked up.

Don't Dwell on Missed Opportunities or Wait for Them

If you don't give yourself enough lead time to tell the story, then you have a wasted a PR opportunity. You should always give yourself at least one month if not two to prep for a news or product release. This prep includes who, what, and where to pitch. If you do miss an opportunity, don't dwell on it. There will always be other opportunities for press.

Waiting for that perfect PR storm is also a mistake since PR is something that is more art than science. You might not know what will work for your organization until you start doing it, so put stuff out there, make mistakes and learn from them.

The best thing to do is get your system down, make sure your press kit is up-to-date, and build relationships with the reporters that cover your space so that you can help them, help you get great press.

Ways to Take Action Now!

1. **Refresh Your Reporter List:** Remember that list of reporters I told you to follow? Take a look at those reporters and see if you need to remove or add more. Reporters frequently change beats.

2. **Refresh Your Editorial Calendar:** Each month, refresh your editorial calendar to take into account any changes. It's vital that you always be looking to build up capacity and adjust to the news cycle.

3. **Subscribe to Email Newsletters:** The best way to stay on top of current events is to sign up for industry email newsletters like The Hustle, CB Insights, PR Week, and Inside Daily. Email newsletters are a wealth of information and can give you valuable insights into what's going on.

7

Secret #7: The Line Between PR & Marketing Is Blurry

Even though you feel your organization is the most amazing thing in the world, it doesn't mean a reporter will, and it certainly doesn't mean that a reporter will write a story about you. Good press has to be earned. One way to earn good press is to have a marketing strategy that complements your PR efforts. This is required with the advent of social media and how it's transformed both marketing and PR. A solid PR strategy needs to include some aspects of marketing, especially social media marketing, or you will leave a lot of great PR opportunities on the table.

Nowadays, you can consider social media a good way to generate PR opportunities since lots of stories, posts, and pictures go viral without having to pitch them to reporters or media outlets. This makes it even more important that your social media marketing strategy have a PR component. At the very least, you'll need to have a strategy when your social media posts go viral.

Always Build Relationships

Building relationships with reporters is critical to getting good coverage. Those relationships start by reaching out to them before you need coverage and being helpful when they ask for something. Follow them on social media, share their posts and comment when appropriate. Interact with them periodically so that they know you are active and not just an opportunist.

Even though the Internet is a vast space, our brains have gotten much more impatient, and we now only want to take in the most interesting articles and information before we quickly move on to the next thing. That has made it so reporters will *only* cover the most interesting and compelling topics, from sources they trust. After all, reporters are writing articles for the readers they serve, not for your organization!

Be of Service to Others

Like most humans, reporters like people who are helpful and contribute actively to the community. This service to others is a valuable component of both a PR strategy and a social media marketing strategy. The best PR will be bestowed upon you by others who have found your product or service or cause useful, or by some unique and novel aspect of your organization that a reporter uncovered. This is why being a good community member, within your industry, can set the stage for great PR opportunities.

It's human nature to want to help those who have helped us. Social media marketing, when done right, is a great way to help others by giving them valuable facts and tips to make their lives easier. As you build up your social media and PR credibility, more and more opportunities will come your way simply because you and your organization will be at the top of a reporter's mind, or even better, the top of search results. Win-win for everyone!

Good Social Media Is the New PR

The line between PR and marketing is slowly becoming blurred because of social media. Social media is all about building brand awareness, which is exactly what PR is meant to do. Good social media, like good PR, will build your brand equity so that when a potential customer/supporter wants your product or service or donate to the cause, all the great PR and social media you have accumulated over the years will pay off.

To be clear, PR is not marketing's redheaded stepchild. You still have to have a solid PR strategy to augment your social media marketing strategy to create those moments that will raise awareness for your brand, organization, and founders.

Good PR professionals and firms know that social media will never replace PR. PR will always be the best way for a company to get the word out about it's products, services, or causes. A solid social media marketing strategy will make getting reporters to cover you a whole lot easier. Make sure that your campaigns have both a PR and social media component. It will pay off big time in the long run.

Ways to Take Action Now!

1. **Update Your Editorial Calendar with Social Media:** If you have not already added social media to your editorial calendar, now is a good time to do so. Coordinate with

your marketing group so that the message is consistent.

2. **Run a Social Media PR Experiment:** Pick some aspect of your organization and run a social media PR experiment to see how much coverage you can get. This can be as simple as a giveaway or a survey you want people to fill out.

3. **Refresh Your Message:** It is always good to refresh your PR and marketing message in relation to new trends or directions. My advice is to look at it every six months or so.

II

How Tos

"People do not buy goods and services. They buy relations, stories, and magic."
– Seth Godin, Best–Selling Author

8

How to Write Your PR Narrative

An infant child looks at his mother through big, bold eyes and utters his first word: "Mama." An elderly woman takes her last breath as her daughter holds her hand near her bedside as she slowly fades from existence. A crippled soldier receives a medal of honor after sacrificing his limbs to save his buddies. All of these stories move people to feel something and feeling something, is what moves people to take action.

People Love a Good Story

People feast on a story with tragedy and triumph because it creates the empathy that we all desire. It gives people the ability to share the feelings and emotions of the characters, and it resonates with our human morality by channeling our innate desire to feel connected to someone else. It's these ups and downs the the hero's journey that make golden PR moments.

In PR, narrative offers a way to give meaning to ideas, opinions, and values. A narrative can express ideas within a broader framework far better than what corporate slogans.

Slogans can't make a real human connection.

A great story is woven into the fundamental concepts of traditional society and joins together our interpersonal relationships. Good PR makes your organization that much more real and appealing in the public eye.

What Is a PR Narrative?

Your PR narrative is the external story of your organization or movement. It's akin to your organization's narrative but it is primarily focused on developing a relationship with your customers, audience, or supporters. Your PR narrative has to show what you can do for your customers or followers and make them believe that they need you instead of you needing them. Having a strong PR narrative drives your credibility and creates relevance – two things all organizations want.

All Stories Follow a Formula

Shaun Coyne, author of *The Story Grid*, is an editor who has spent his career helping writers tell stories that work. *The Story Grid* framework allows a writer to understand what works and what does not in a story.

One of his fundamental concepts is that stories have three macro parts: the beginning hook, middle build, and ending payoff. All stories, no matter how long or short, need to have these three components. This is exactly how we will build the PR narrative for your company. We'll do that by answering the following three questions:

Question #1: Why Does Your Organization Exist (Beginning Hook)?

Your organization has to have a reason for existing. This reason has to be something that moves people to want to learn more. Ideally, your organization's *Why* is mission driven and contributes to the common good. Having a *Why* to just make money or raise money, etc., will not move people.

When you think about this, consider the reasons you as the founder created the organization. Look deep in your heart to figure out what motivates you to get up every day to make things happen.

Question #2: How is Your Organization Unique (Middle Build)?

In order to succeed, you have to stand out. There are many organizations just like you, but what separates you from them is what makes you unique. You have to know this because if you don't know, how are your customers or supporters going to know? You must explain everything that your organization does and why people need to pay attention to you. Leave no stone unturned.

Question #3: What Pain Does Your Organization Solve (Ending Payoff)?

This is where you close the deal. How do you make sure that your customers or supporters or clients feel like they are getting value for supporting of your organization? How can you fix a problem that they may have? In order to get your customer or donor on board, you must benefit them. You have to be able to show that you can make their lives easier, whether it be by a product you offer or a specified service. What do they gain out of the relationship?

This is the most important for donors. Contrary to your gut feelings, donors want something out of donating to your organization. They might recognize that you are helping many people, but they also care about how donating makes them feel and also how it benefits them. I know it seems counterintuitive but it's true.

Putting It All Together

Now that we have all the pieces to the puzzle, we can construct the narrative in a clear and compelling way. Make sure you read your pieces, edit them for spelling and grammar, and firm up your content. If you think you've got something pretty good, read it aloud and see how it sounds. Reading it aloud is a great way to check for those tricky grammar mistakes and to verify the overall tone of your narrative. It is also a great way to see if you have clearly communicated your vision. If it sounds like the voice you are trying to portray, then you have a good starting point.

Your PR narrative will be the beginning hook (question 1), middle build (question 2), and ending payoff (question 3) above. Of course, the three might not fit exactly together, so make sure to read it aloud and edit when necessary. It's essential that each component of the narrative be present so that your potential customers or donors know why you do what you do, how you stand out, and what pain you solve.

JSY PR & Marketing's PR Narrative

To give you an idea of what a PR narrative is all about, here is the PR narrative for JSY PR & Marketing:

JSY PR & Marketing harnesses the power of media to affect positive change for our clients. Our approach takes the best of what an organization has to offer and amplifies it through creative uses of PR. We help clients navigate the turbulent seas of media so that they can take full advantage of their place in the world.

9

How to Hire the Right PR Firm

Our organizations are our babies, and when we need help, we all feel a little vulnerable. So if you're ready to hire a PR firm, then you should hire one that is willing to run through the fire to rescue your baby. Well, not exactly but they should be willing to rescue you from bad PR situations and to nurture your organization along. How can you figure out which firm is the best choice?

It's Kinda Like Dating

Hiring a PR firm, actually hiring any outside contractor, is like dating: You never know how someone will be after the courtship phase. Most people are on their best behaviors when they meet someone new, and that means you might not get a true sense of how they will work with you until later. Like dating, it's always best to get a recommendation from someone you trust who can tell you the inside story of how the firm (or person) actually behaves. It's also important to follow your gut, and make sure you see the warning signs and are not blinded by reputation.

Questions to Ask and Traps to Avoid

Picking the right PR firm will be an important step in your company's evolution. Consider asking the questions below to get to know a potential PR firm:

- **Are you ready for PR?** Before you go off and interview a firm, make sure you're ready to hire someone.
- **Do they have experience in your field?** It is important that a firm knows your organization and the major players in it.
- **What do they know about your company?** Directly ask them about your company to gauge if they understand what business you are in.
- **Ask them five reasons they want to work with you:** The five reasons test is a great way to see how much homework a firm has done on your company and what ideas they might have to make you successful.
- **Can they commit to weekly company meetings?** Team interaction is critical to a successful relationship with a PR firm, and that starts with regular meetings to give status updates as well as discuss ideas.
- **How will they communicate with the team?** Communication is paramount, and the way a firm communicates with clients says a lot about the firms work style. Is it open and loose, or rigid and formal or spotty?
- **Will they give you monthly reports?** Monthly reports can be useful for metrics and status updates so that everything is documented and tracked.
- **Are they willing to come on site or go to a team offsite?** Face time is important to build rapport. Some decisions are better made in person where ideas and strategies can be debated and discussed.

- **How much of your staff time is required to manage them?** Someone on your staff will need to be the interface between the PR and your company. It's best to find out how much effort that will take.

I'm sure you can come up with several other questions to answer but I thought I would give you a few to get your mind thinking. When you listen to the responses, see if the answers are canned and can be the response for any old company. Again, trust your gut on this. Along with the questions above, there are also some traps to avoid when picking a firm and interacting with them. Those traps include:

- **Don't Do PR by Projects:** It's best to have a firm on retainer because then they are more part of the team. PR is not a one and done project. It's a continuum that always needs care and feeding. With that said, you can have project based events or campaigns but make sure you figure out the success metrics first.
- **Set Realistic Metrics:** Metrics are vital to set early because they will set the tone for the interactions and expectations. Some metrics to consider are: story coverage, social media reach, article placement, etc.
- **Be Realistic:** PR is more art than science. Sure, you can put out a press release but sometimes, coverage in the media can go through a dry spell. Knowing the reasons for the dry spell is important, and your firm should be able to give you some insights.
- **Do Check References:** I'm shocked at how many companies don't check references at their own peril. It's also wise to check back-channel references as well.
- **Ask Who Will Manage Your Account:** Some firms will

promise that a senior partner will manage your account, but in reality, it's usually a junior associate. Watch out for this trap and make sure you understand who will manage your account and how much mind share you will get.

At the end of the day, you want a firm that will cater to your unique needs. See if the firm is open to listening to your ideas and concerns. A good PR firm will be an extension of your team and if you are not feeling that, then they are the wrong choice for you.

10

How to Pitch a Reporter

I'm sure most of my fellow PR mavens will be a little upset with me that I'm letting you in on the secret of the fine art of pitching a reporter. To them, I'd say "relax" since revealing this will only make us more valuable. If you don't believe me, then read on my skeptical friend.

I have given this advice a thousand times and it still shocks me that most founders don't listen. All founders pitch reporters wrong. This makes my job and every other PR maven's job a lot harder. Let me explain.

Like most things in PR, pitching a reporter is more art than science. Reporters actually like hearing from founders because they get to interact directly with a source – a big plus to get the inside scoop. The problem is that most founders are so in love with what they do that they tend to take things personally, give too much information, and hold grudges. PR mavens like me will always have a job – we know how to do the dance.

Elements of a Perfect Pitch

Did I hype this enough? I hope so because out of all the things a PR professional does, the pitch is the most important. In fact, what I'm about to describe works for all types of pitches, be it for a reporter or a new product or a new program. The reason is simple.

The sole job of the pitch is to get the next level of interaction going, either an email or a phone call or a meeting. It's job is to continue the conversation. You need to do just enough to peak interest – nothing more, nothing less. This is the art of the pitch.

To help you formulate the perfect pitch, consider below the essential elements of a pitch that gets a response:

- **Snappy Subject:** The subject line of your pitch is just like the subject of a story. It has to compel the reader to want more. It also needs to convey if the information is embargoed or time sensitive. An embargo is the date that news will be released to the general public.
- **Personal Connection:** Don't ever and I repeat *ever* send spam out to a list of reporters. They will discard it right away. Rather, make your communication personal and let them know you follow what they cover.
- **Short and Sweet:** A pitch should be no more than three to four short, snappy paragraphs. That's it. That's all. Bullet points are even better. Any more than that is a waste of typing.
- **Don't Attach Anything:** A first pitch is a teaser. It is meant to peak the reporters interest. If they want more, they will ask for it.
- **Clear Call to Action:** Make sure you tell them what your

desired result is. Something like: Can I count on you to cover this? This makes it crystal clear what you want.

I cannot stress this enough since *every* founder *never* takes this advice. Keep the pitch short and sweet. Reporters are busy and if you send them a long email, they will rightfully discard it. Repeat after me: short and sweet.

When and How to Pitch

Now that you know how to prepare the perfect pitch, you are now going to have to send it out. Remember those 10 or so reporters you're following on social media? I hope you also found their emails since those are the people to whom you're going to pitch.

To get the maximum exposure for your pitch, make sure you follow these simple rules:

1. **Pitch Reporters at Specific Times:** The basic rule of thumb is that you only pitch reporters on Tuesday through Thursday. Preferably in the morning. The reason is Mondays and Fridays are spent either in editorial meetings or finishing up stories. Of course, there are exceptions to this, specifically when it comes to breaking news.

2. **Follow up Aggressively, but Politely:** Don't feel too bad about following up a lot. Reporters are busy and they sometimes forget just like all of us. Be respectful but also be aggressive. What I mean by aggressive is once a day; that's about the level of aggression that makes sense for a pitch follow-up.

3. **Don't Pitch Outlets at the Same Time:** Many a newbie has made this mistake and it makes things a little weird.

Reporters, like all of us, talk. In some cases, they might even sit right next to each other. This means you should only pitch one of them at an outlet (e.g. publication) unless you specifically say who else you pitched and why.

4. **Have Follow-Up Materials Ready:** Make sure that you have all follow-up materials ready to go when a reporter follows up. This includes times and dates for executive interviews if required.

It's *Way* Harder than It Sounds

Looks simple, right? It's actually a lot harder than it looks and quite time consuming. That's one of the reasons why PR professionals and reporters like working together; we understand the process and know what each other needs.

You as founders can and should pitch reporters but not without the help of a PR professional who can help craft your pitch, get the materials ready, and follow up as needed. That will go a long way in getting reporters to cover you.

11

How to Build Your PR Capacity

Many organizations come to me in a panic because they have a PR opportunity and zero idea how to handle it. This frustrates me because I really want to help them, but there's often not enough time or not enough material to take advantage of the luck that just dropped in their lap.

That's why it's important to understand and implement the ideas in this book so that you have PR capacity when an opportunity comes your way. The worst feeling in the world, trust me on this, is a missed PR opportunity because you're not set up to handle it.

What Exactly Is PR Capacity?

PR capacity is your organization's ability to capitalize on a PR event. These PR events can include a product launch, raising money, breaking news, or fundraiser. The whole goal behind building this capacity is so that you can focus on getting the message right without worrying about the message, channel, narrative, etc.

The time to build your PR capacity is when you don't need

it. Think of PR capacity as training in the gym for a sport. You train before the big game because without training you're going to perform poorly.

Ways to Build PR Capacity

PR capacity is something that has to be constantly worked on. It's not something you can do a month or even six months before a product launch. You have to take it just as seriously as you do your sales and marketing efforts because you never know when some PR opportunity will pop up.

In order to effectively build your organizations PR capacity, consider the following tasks:

- **Implement All the Ways to Take Action:** This should go without saying but I'll say it anyway. Make sure to read through everything in this book.
- **Create a PR Cadence:** The best way to build PR capacity is to do PR. I mean, c'mon, there must be something worth talking about. Get out there and make things happen!
- **Start Blogging:** I'm always shocked to see how many companies don't blog about what they do. That is the single best way to get found on Google, which in turn gets you found by reporters since, duh, reporters use Google all the time.
- **Be a Thought Leader:** The best way to get reporters to want to cover you and your company is to be an expert or thought leader in a particular field or market. This requires giving talks, writing books, blog posting, etc.

An Example of Stellar PR Capacity

We worked with a humanitarian aid organization whose goal was to raise money to support healthcare in worn torn countries via their parent organization based in Europe.

When the San Francisco based office first hired us, they had a vision as to how to get the word out about the work they did. This was especially important because they did not have a big presence in the United States.

For over six months, we worked with them to throw events, raise funds, and reach out to reporters who covered international healthcare. This capacity to know the players in your space and to have a constant drumbeat of coverage would pay off in a big way.

2014 Ebola Outbreak in West Africa

In the summer of 2014, Ebola was ravaging West Africa. Particularly hard hit was Sierra Leone. The global focus on the crisis and the lack of information made it a challenge to know what was going on.

During the crisis, this organization had the only fully functioning hospital in all of Sierra Leone and that caused reporters to go to them as a source for developments on the ground.

Because they had built up a PR capacity to handle such a circumstance, their Executive Director was constantly fielding major news outlet requests for interviews. This increased the awareness of the crisis and positioned them as not only the go to source for the latest information but it highlighted the important work they were doing. This organization would not have been able to handle such an opportunity without building up a PR capacity as the go-to source for global health issues in Sierra Leone.

Always Be Prepared

This example is one of many in which a client has built up the capacity to take advantage of an opportunity. Being prepared for a breaking PR event is at the heart of building PR capacity. If they had not built up their PR capacity over the preceding six months, no one would have known that the organization was on the ground and helping people. That's why it's vital to have a PR cadence that builds your capacity to be of service to society when breaking news strikes.

Conclusion

So there you have it! Those are the 7 *PR Secrets All Founders Should Know* along with some *How To's* to help you get some PR. This book is just the start and should get you thinking about how to harness the power of PR for your organization.

I hope you implement some of these secrets and also pay closer attention to how your organization's PR is being run. PR is a necessity for all organizations. Being able to build your organization's PR capacity will serve you and your organization well. Strive to be a good community member and to have a constant cadence of PR to make sure your organization is ready and relevant.

Don't be afraid to take on the challenge of generating PR for your organization. PR can be a lot of fun and you will see results if you work at it long enough. Now, get out there and pitch, pitch, pitch!

Acknowledgements

Thanks to all my friends, family, and clients for their support over the years. Thanks to Sarah Prejean for her kind ear and valuable insights. Eric Talbert for his insights into the non-profit world.

Thanks to Tallie and Tom Fishburne for the use of the front cover cartoon. I really enjoy Tom's cartoons and the one on the cover captures exactly the challenge of PR.

Thanks to Lily at Bllew photography for the beautiful author headshot.

Special thanks to my husband Jarie for helping me put together the "7 PR Secrets" email series and for being by my side through thick and thin. I am grateful for your partnership and love.

About the Authors

Jane Yin Bolander (March 2, 1981 – April 3, 2017) was the founder and CEO of JSY PR and Marketing, a firm that helped professional athletes, non-profits, and startups tell their story. She had over fifteen years of PR and Marketing experience and had been running JSY PR & Marketing for over twelve years. Her clients included celebrities such as Dontari Poe, Amare Stoudemire, Lance Briggs, Anna Rawson, and Amel Larrieux.

Jane was an advocate for minority and women owned businesses. She would often volunteer to coach and mentor them. She had a particular passion for stopping human trafficking via her work with the Bay Area Anti-Trafficking Collation. She was a loving daughter, devoted friend, and caring wife who was taken from us way too soon.

Jarie Bolander is an engineer by training and an entrepreneur by nature with over twenty years of bringing innovative solutions to market, such as Bluetooth, USB, RFID, and Semiconductor DNA sequencing. He is currently the co-founder and COO of Lab Sensor Solutions, a digital health company that is applying sensor technology to track the temperature and location of clinical samples to prevent spoilage. He is also now the principal at JSY PR & Marketing.

Jarie has formed or been part of six startups in various management roles. He holds an MBA in Technology Management from UOP and a BS in Electrical Engineering from San Jose

State University. He is also an inventor or co-inventor who holds over ten patents and has published three books. These books are: *Frustration Free Technical Management*; *#ENDURANCE tweet — A Little Nudge to Keep You Going*; and *Business Basics for Entrepreneurs*.